Edvard
GREIG

LYRIC SUITE
Op.54
Edited by
Richard W. Sargeant, Jr.

Study Score
Partitur

SERENISSIMA MUSIC, INC.

ORCHESTRA

Piccolo

2 Flutes

2 Oboes

2 Clarinets (B-flat and A)

2 Bassoons

4 Horns (F)

2 Trumpets (C)*

3 Trombones

Tuba

Timpani

Percussion

Harp

Violin I

Violin II

Viola

Violoncello

Double Bass

*The present score has been updated for the commonkeys of modern instruments
(Clarinets in A or B-flat, Horns in F, Trumpets in C). The original score featured
Trumpets in F in both Seidl's 1894 orchestration and Grieg's 1904 reworking.

Duration: ca. 17 minutes

Premiere: April 1906
Amsterdam
Concertgebouw Theatre
Royal Concertgebouw Orchestra / Composer

ISMN: 979-0-58042-109-8
This score is anewly-engraved edition based upon the composer's manuscript, of which
four movements were a reworking of Anton Seidl's 1894 orchestration, and the first edition
full score and parts issued ca.1905 by C.F. Peters of Leipzig.

Printed in the USA
First Printing: August, 2018

LYRIC SUITE
Op. 54

1. Gjætergut
(Shepherd's Boy)

Edvard Grieg
Edited by Richard W. Sargeant, Jr.

Andantino espressive ♪. = 48

Harp

Andantino espressive ♪. = 48

Violin 1

Violin 2

Viola

Violoncello

Contrabass

17 poco mosso

Hp.

17 poco mosso

Vn. 1

2

Va.

Vc.

Cb.

42219

18
Hp.
p
mf
p
Vn.
1
2
Va.
Vc.
Cb.
rubato
rubato
24
string.
28
rall.
mf
cresc.
f
dim.
cresc. sempre
rubato
rubato
f
dim.
div.
cresc. sempre
f
dim.
non div.
div.
cresc. sempre
f
dim.
unis.
cresc. sempre
f
dim.

31
Hp.
31
Vn.
1
2
Va.
Vc.
Cb.
p
pp
f
div.

38 Tempo I
Hp.
f
p
38 Tempo I
Vn.
1
2
Va.
Vc.
Cb.
unis.
f
pp

46 poco mosso
44
Hp.
f
p
46 poco mosso
44
div.
1
Vn.
2
Va.
Vc.
Cb.
fp
rubato
49
mf
p
rubato

stretto
57
54
Hp.
cresc.
f
stretto
57
54
rubato cresc.
rubato
Vn.
1
2
Va.
Vc.
Cb.
cresc.
f
rall.
59
Hp.
dim.
p
pp
rall.
59
dim.
p
pp
div.

Tempo I
71
66
Hp.
ff
p
Tempo I
71
66
Vn.
unis.
div.
Va.
Vc.
Cb.
fz
Agitato
73
cresc. molto
ffz

79 meno
78
Hp.
mp
79 meno
78
Vn.
1
2
Va.
Vc.
Cb.
dim.
4
p
unis.
84
Hp.
ppp
84
Vn. 1
Vn. 2
con sord.
div. a 4
con sord.
div. a 3
pp
unis.
p tranq.
div.

2. Klokkeklang
(Bell Ringing)

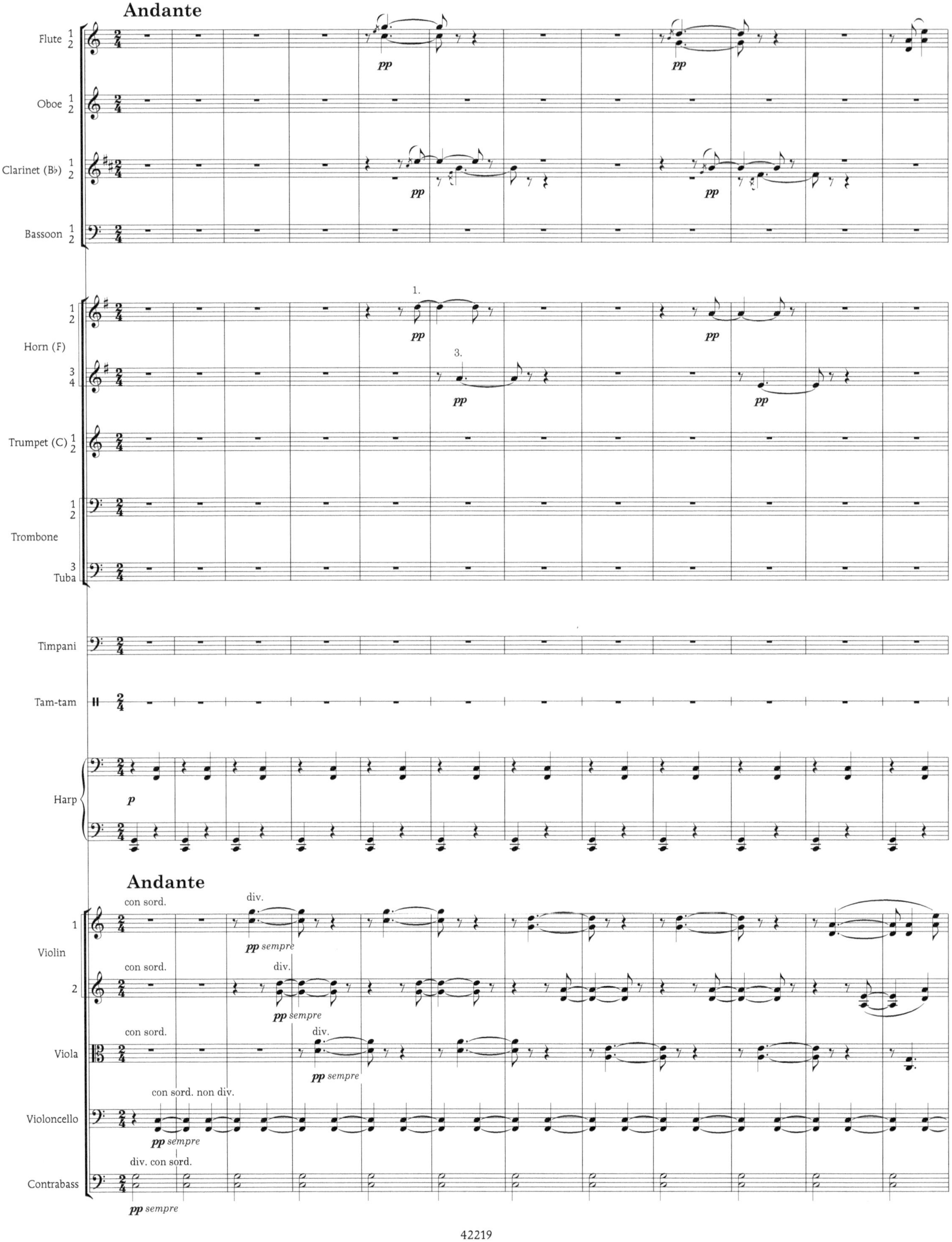

13
19
Fl. 1 2
very tender
pp
Ob. 1 2
pp very tender
Cl. 1 2
pp very tender
pp
Bn. 1 2
pp
Hn. 1 2
(1.)
pp
3 4
(3.)
pp
Tpt. 1 2
Trb. 1 2
3
Tuba
Timp.
T.-t.
Hp.
p
13
19
Vn. 1
pp sempre
2
unis.
pp sempre
Va.
div.
pp sempre
Vc.
div.
Cb.

25
Fl. 1 2
pp
very tender
Ob. 1 2
pp very tender
Cl. 1 2
pp
pp very tender
Bn. 1 2
pp
Hn. 1 2
pp
3 4
pp
Tpt. 1 2
Trb. 1 2
3 Tuba
Timp.
T.-t.
Hp.
25
Vn. 1
2
unis.
Va.
Vc.
Cb.

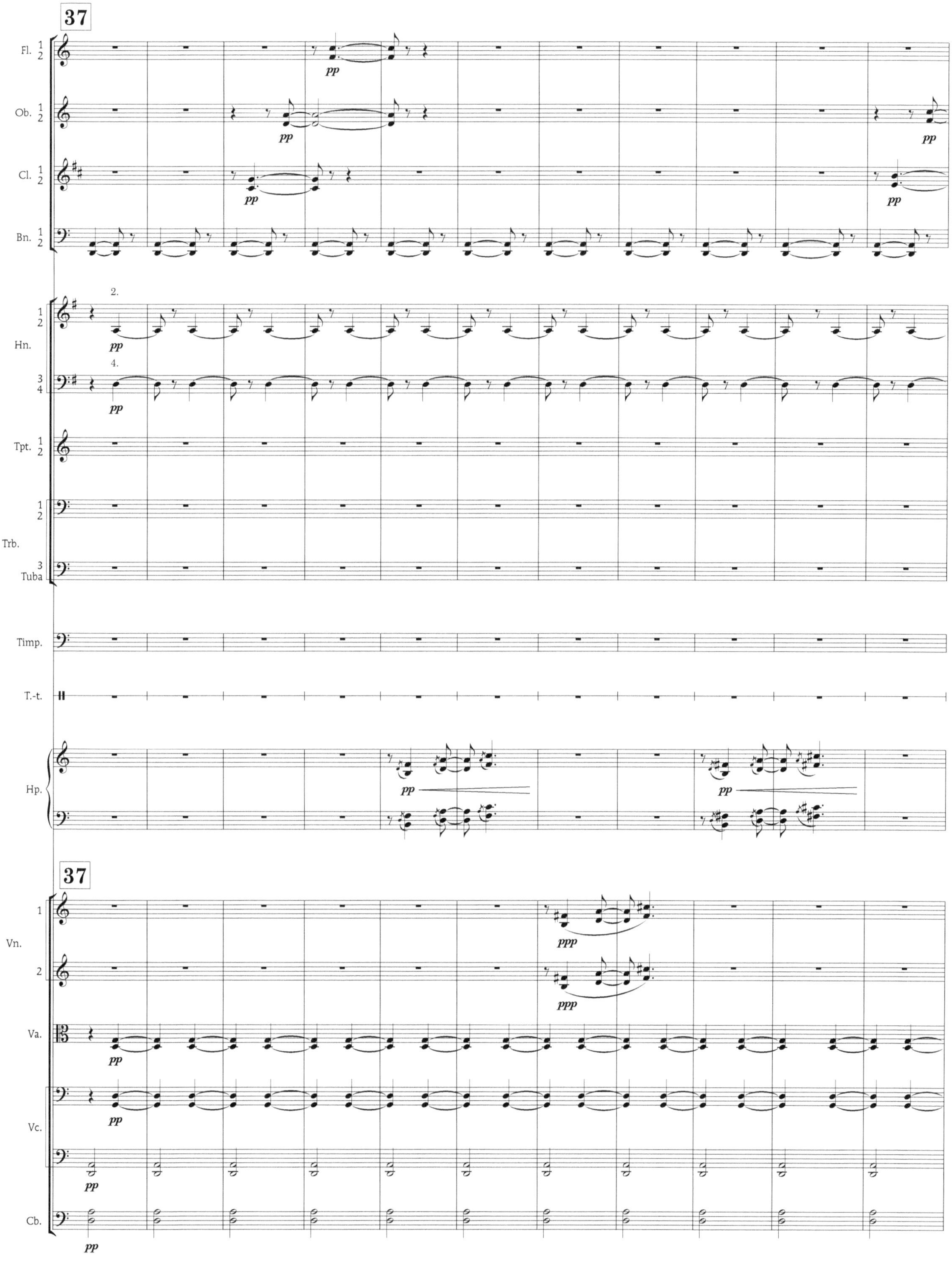
37
Fl. 1 2
pp
Ob. 1 2
pp
pp
Cl. 1 2
pp
pp
Bn. 1 2
Hn. 1 2
2.
pp
3 4
4.
pp
Tpt. 1 2
Trb. 1 2
3 Tuba
Timp.
T.-t.
Hp.
pp
pp
37
Vn. 1
ppp
2
ppp
Va.
pp
Vc.
pp
pp
Cb.
pp

48
55
Fl. 1 2
pp
Ob. 1 2
Cl. 1 2
Bn. 1 2
Hn. 1 2
3 4
Tpt. 1 2
Trb. 1 2
3 Tuba
Timp.
T.-t.
pp
Hp.
pp
pp
p cresc.
48
55
Vn. 1
ppp
p cresc. poco a poco
2
ppp
p cresc. poco a poco
Va.
cresc. poco a poco
Vc.
cresc. poco a poco
cresc. poco a poco
Cb.
cresc. poco a poco

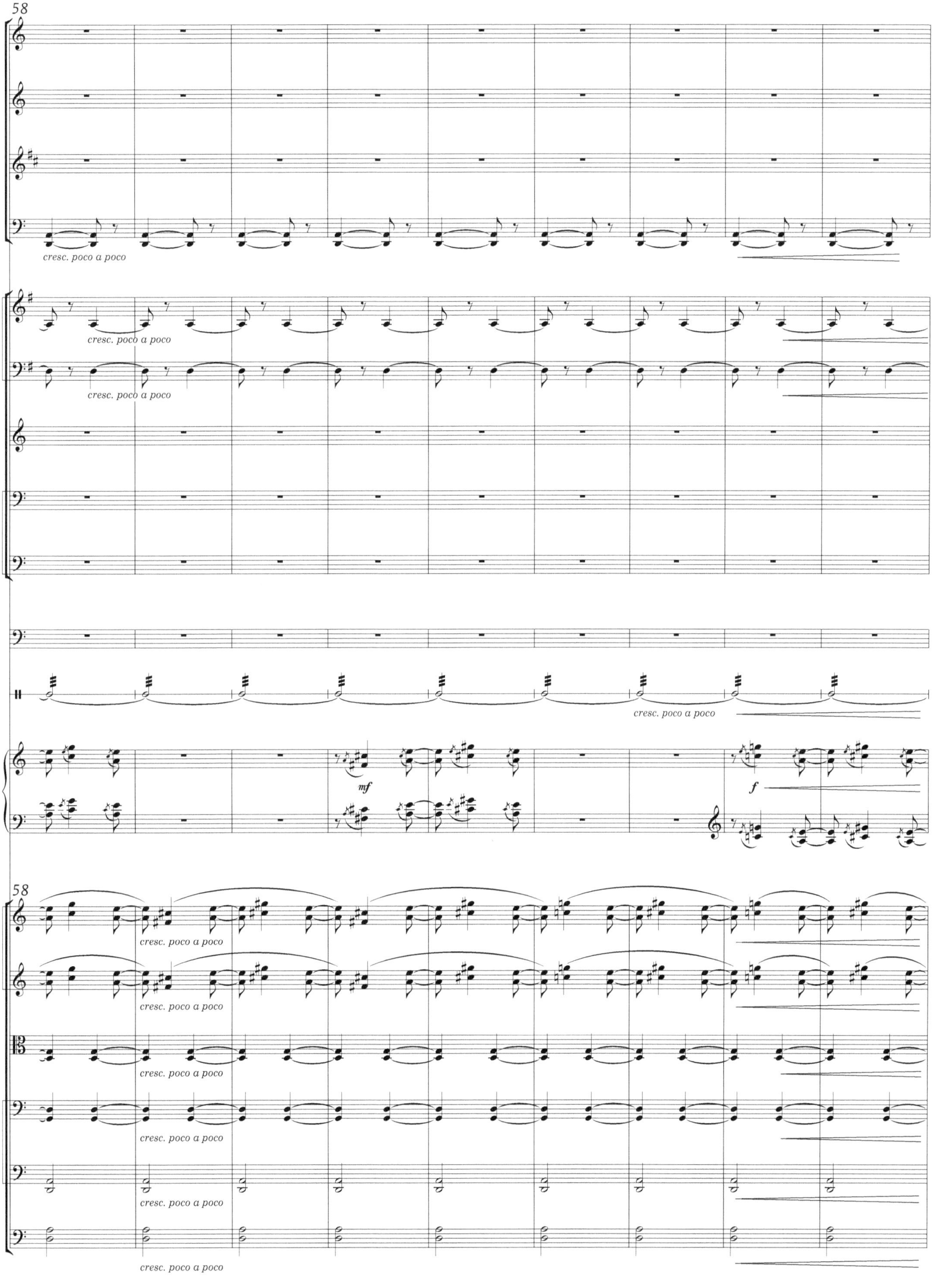
58
Fl. 1 2
Ob. 1 2
Cl. 1 2
Bn. 1 2
cresc. poco a poco
Hn. 1 2 3 4
cresc. poco a poco
cresc. poco a poco
Tpt. 1 2
Trb. 1 2 3
Tuba
Timp.
T.-t.
cresc. poco a poco
Hp.
mf
f
58
Vn. 1 2
cresc. poco a poco
cresc. poco a poco
Va.
cresc. poco a poco
Vc.
cresc. poco a poco
cresc. poco a poco
Cb.
cresc. poco a poco

67
poco rit.
Fl.
Ob.
Cl.
Bn.
Hn.
Tpt.
Trb.
Tuba
Timp.
T.-t.
Hp.
Vn.
Va.
Vc.
Cb.
unis.
fff
dim.
fz
p
pp
ppp
mf

78
Tempo I
Fl. 1 2
Ob. 1 2
Cl. 1 2
Bn. 1 2
Hn. 1 2 3 4
Tpt. 1 2
Trb. 1 2 3
Tuba
Timp.
T.-t.
Hp.
p
dim.
78
Tempo I
Vn. 1 2
pp
senza sord.
Va.
pizz.
p
Vc.
Cb.

18

G. P. 95

G. P. 95

42219

99
Fl. 1 2
Ob. 1 2
Cl. 1 2
to A cl.
Bn. 1 2
ff
dim.
Hn. 1 2
2.
p
pp
ppp
3 4
4.
Tpt. 1 2
Trb. 1 2
3
Tuba
Timp.
T.-t.
l.v.
Hp.
Vn. 1
2
Va.
fff
senza sord.
Vc.
Cb.
pizz.
arco

3. Gangar

Allegretto marcato ♩. = 92
Flute 1 2
Oboe 1 2
Clarinet (A) 1 2
Bassoon 1 2
Horn (F) 1 2 3 4
Trumpet (C) 1 2
Trombone 1 2 3
Tuba
Timpani
Harp
Allegretto marcato ♩. = 92
Violin 1 2
Viola
Violoncello
Contrabass
pizz.
p
ffp
f

9
Fl. 1 2
Ob. 1 2
Cl. 1 2
Bn. 1 2
ffp
Hn. 1 2
ffp
3 4
ffp
Tpt. 1 2
Trb. 1 2
3 Tuba
Timp.
f
Hp.
mf
mf
p
9
Vn. 1
arco
p
2
arco
fp
Va.
arco
fp
Vc.
div. arco
fp
Cb.
arco
fp
div.

17
18
Fl. 1 2
Ob. 1 2
Cl. 1 2
Bn. 1 2
a2
ff
p
2.
1.
Hn. 1 2
Hn. 3 4
Tpt. 1 2
Trb. 1 2
3 Tuba
Timp.
Hp.
Vn. 1
Vn. 2
Va.
Vc.
Cb.
unis.
pizz. div.
arco unis.
pizz.

24
29
Fl. 1 2
Ob. 1 2
a2
cresc.
1.
p
Cl. 1 2
a2
1.
Bn. 1 2
2.
pp
Hn.
1 2
3 4
Tpt. 1 2
Trb.
1 2
3
Tuba
Timp.
Hp.
pizz.
div.
div. a3
Vn. 1
Vn. 2
pizz. div.
Va.
Vc.
arco
Cb.

31
Fl. 1 2
Ob. 1 2
dim.
Cl. 1 2
dim.
pp
Bn. 1 2
dim.
pp
1 2
Hn.
dim.
ppp
3 4
dim.
ppp
Tpt. 1 2
1 2
Trb.
3
Tuba
Timp.
Hp.
pp
31
Vn. 1
dim.
pp
Vn. 2
dim.
pp
Va.
dim.
pp
Vc.
dim.
pp
Cb.
dim.
pp

41
40
1.
pp
Fl. 1 2
Ob. 1 2
Cl. 1 2
Bn. 1 2
Hn. 1 2
3 4
Tpt. 1 2
Trb. 1 2
3
Tuba
Timp.
Hp.
p
8va
41
40
div. a2
arco
arco unis.
pp
Vn. 1
2
Va.
Vc.
Cb.

48
53
Fl. 1 2
a2
mf
Ob. 1 2
Cl. 1 2
1.
p
Bn. 1 2
Hn. 1 2
3 4
Tpt. 1 2
Trb. 1 2
3 Tuba
Timp.
Hp.
(8)
cresc.
Vn. 1
2
cresc.
mf più marc. sempre
Va.
Vc.
Cb.

56
Fl. 1 2
cresc.
f
cresc.
Ob. 1 2
cresc.
f
cresc.
Cl. 1 2
cresc.
f
cresc.
Bn. 1 2
Hn. 1 2
3 4
Tpt. 1 2
Trb. 1 2
3
Tuba
Timp.
Hp.
ff
56
Vn. 1
(with a broad stroke)
f
2
(with a broad stroke)
f
Va.
arco unis.
f
cresc.
ff pesante
Vc.
arco (div.)
ff pesante
Cb.
arco
ff pesante

64
69 Etwas schwerer (poco più pesante)
a2
Fl. 1 2
Ob. 1 2
Cl. 1 2
Bn. 1 2
ff
Hn. 1 2 3 4
ff
ff
Tpt. 1 2
Trb. 1 2 3
Tuba
Timp.
Hp.
ff
69 Etwas schwerer (poco più pesante)
64
unison non div.
Vn. 1 2
ff
non div.
ff
non div.
Va.
ff
unison non div.
Vc.
ff
Cb.
ff

72
Fl. 1 2
Ob. 1 2
Cl. 1 2
Bn. 1 2
a2
Hn. 1 2 3 4
a2
Tpt. 1 2
Trb. 1 2 3
Tuba
Timp.
Hp.
dim.
72
Vn. 1 2
Va.
Vc.
Cb.
pizz.
arco
dim.

85
81
Fl. 1 2
Ob. 1 2
Cl. 1 2
Bn. 1 2
Hn. 1 2 3 4
Tpt. 1 2
Trb. 1 2 3
Tuba
Timp.
Hp.
Vn. 1 2
Va.
Vc.
Cb.
a2
2.
unis.
pizz. div.
pizz.

89
Fl. 1 2
Ob. 1 2
Cl. 1 2
Bn. 1 2
Hn. 1 2
3 4
Tpt. 1 2
Trb. 1 2
3 Tuba
Timp.
Hp.
Vn. 1
2
Va.
Vc.
Cb.
ff
p
1.
a2
cresc.
pizz. div.
arco unis.
arco
pizz.

96
Fl. 1 2
Ob. 1 2
1.
p
dim.
Cl. 1 2
1.
p
dim.
pp
Bn. 1 2
2.
pp
dim.
Hn. 1 2
pp
dim.
ppp
3 4
pp
dim.
ppp
Tpt. 1 2
Trb. 1 2
3
Tuba
Timp.
Hp.
96
Vn. 1
div. a3
p
dim.
pp
Vn. 2
div. a3
p
dim.
pp
Va.
p
dim.
pp
Vc.
p
dim.
pp
Cb.
p
dim.
pp

108
104
1.
Fl. 1 2
pp
Ob. 1 2
Cl. 1 2
Bn. 1 2
pp
Hn. 1 2 3 4
Tpt. 1 2
Trb. 1 2 3
Tuba
Timp.
Hp.
pp
p
8va
108
104
arco
Vn. 1
pp
div. a2
arco
pp
arco
Vn. 2
pp
div. a2
arco
pp
pp
pp
Va.
Vc.
Cb.

120
113
Fl. 1 2
a2
mf
Ob. 1 2
a2
mf
Cl. 1 2
1.
p
a2
mf
Bn. 1 2
Hn. 1 2
3 4
Tpt. 1 2
Trb. 1 2
3 Tuba
Timp.
Hp.
(8)
cresc.
113
120
Vn. 1
unis.
cresc.
mf più marc. sempre
2
cresc.
mf più marc. sempre
Va.
Vc.
Cb.

121
Fl. 1 2
Ob. 1 2
Cl. 1 2
Bn. 1 2
Hn. 1 2 3 4
Tpt. 1 2
Trb. 1 2 3
Tuba
Timp.
Hp.
Vn. 1 2
Va.
Vc.
Cb.
cresc.
ff
arco unison
f
ff pesante
arco (div.)
arco

128
a2
Fl. 1 2
f
cresc.
Ob. 1 2
f
cresc.
Cl. 1 2
f
cresc.
Bn. 1 2
ff
Hn. 1 2
ff
3 4
ff
Tpt. 1 2
Trb. 1 2
3 Tuba
Timp.
Hp.
128 (with a broad stroke)
Vn. 1
f
(with a broad stroke)
2
f
Va.
Vc.
Cb.

136 Etwas schwerer (poco più pesante)

136 Etwas schwerer (poco più pesante)

144
151
Fl. 1 2
Ob. 1 2
Cl. 1 2
Bn. 1 2
Hn. 1 2
Hn. 3 4
Tpt. 1 2
Trb. 1 2
3 Tuba
Timp.
Hp.
Vn. 1
2
Va.
Vc.
Cb.
a2
1.
2.
p
f
fp
mf
dim.
pizz.
arco

152
Fl. 1 2
Ob. 1 2
Cl. 1 2
pp
to B♭ cl.
Bn. 1 2
Hn. 1 2
pp
3 4
Tpt. 1 2
Trb. 1 2
3
Tuba
Timp.
pp
Hp.
152
Vn. 1
2
div.
dim.
pp
pizz. unison
Va.
pizz.
Vc.
Cb.
pizz.

4. Notturno

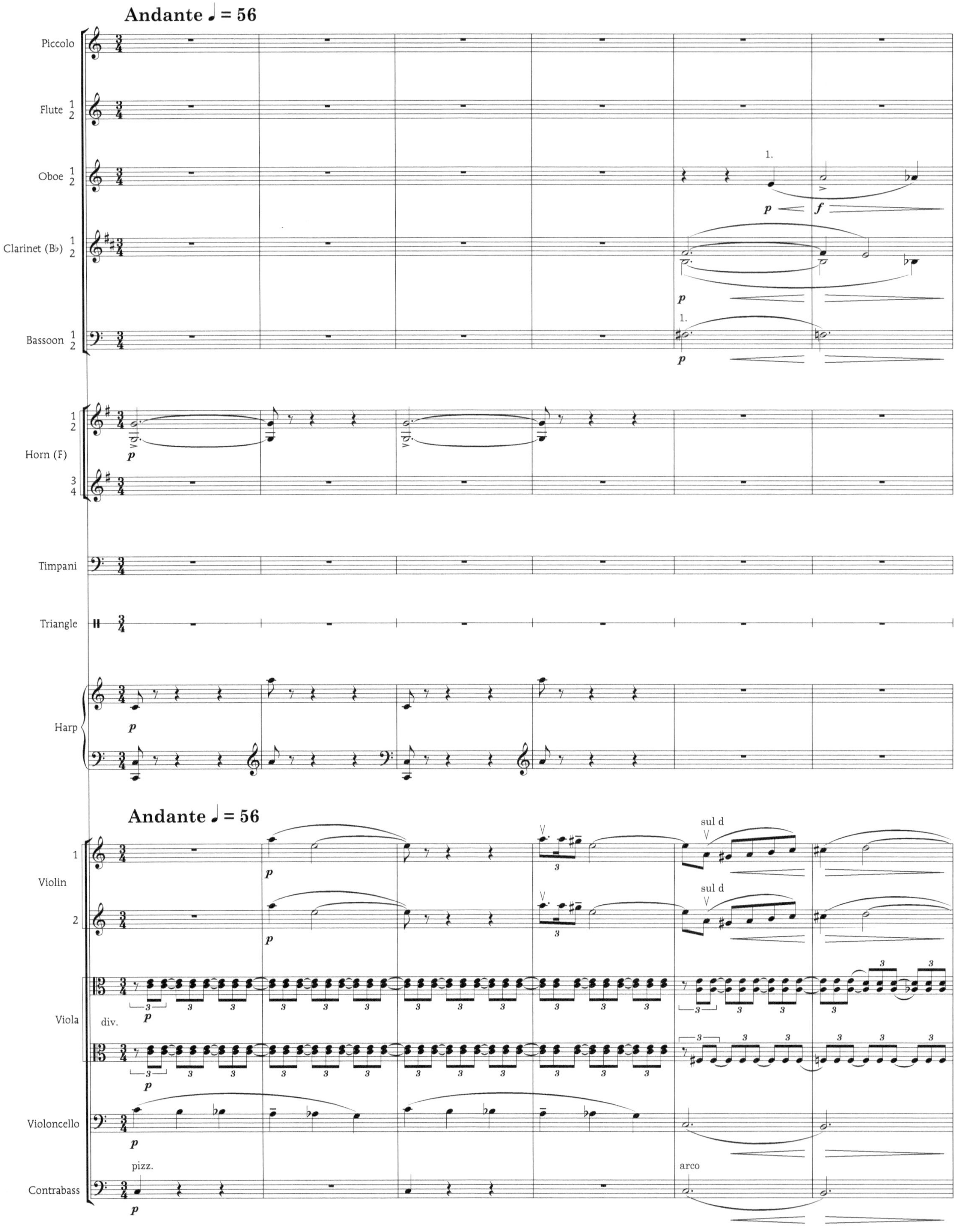
Andante ♩ = 56
Piccolo
Flute 1 2
Oboe 1 2
1.
p
f
Clarinet (B♭) 1 2
p
Bassoon 1 2
1.
p
Horn (F) 1 2 3 4
p
Timpani
Triangle
Harp
p
Andante ♩ = 56
Violin 1 2
p
sul d
Viola
div.
p
Violoncello
p
Contrabass
pizz.
p
arco

7
Picc.
Fl. 1 2
Ob. 1 2
Cl. 1 2
Bn. 1 2
Hn. 1 2 3 4
Timp.
Tgl.
Hp.
Vn. 1 2
Va.
Vc.
Cb.
sul a
sul a
cresc.
più f
div.

15
14
Picc.
Fl. 1 2
1.
pp
6
9
tr
Ob. 1 2
2.
pp
Cl. 1 2
pp
Bn. 1 2
Hn. 1 2
3 4
p
Timp.
Tgl.
Hp.
pp
pp
15
14
div.
Vn. 1
2
pp
pp
Va.
pizz.
p
pizz.
p
Vc.
pizz.
p
Cb.
pizz.
p

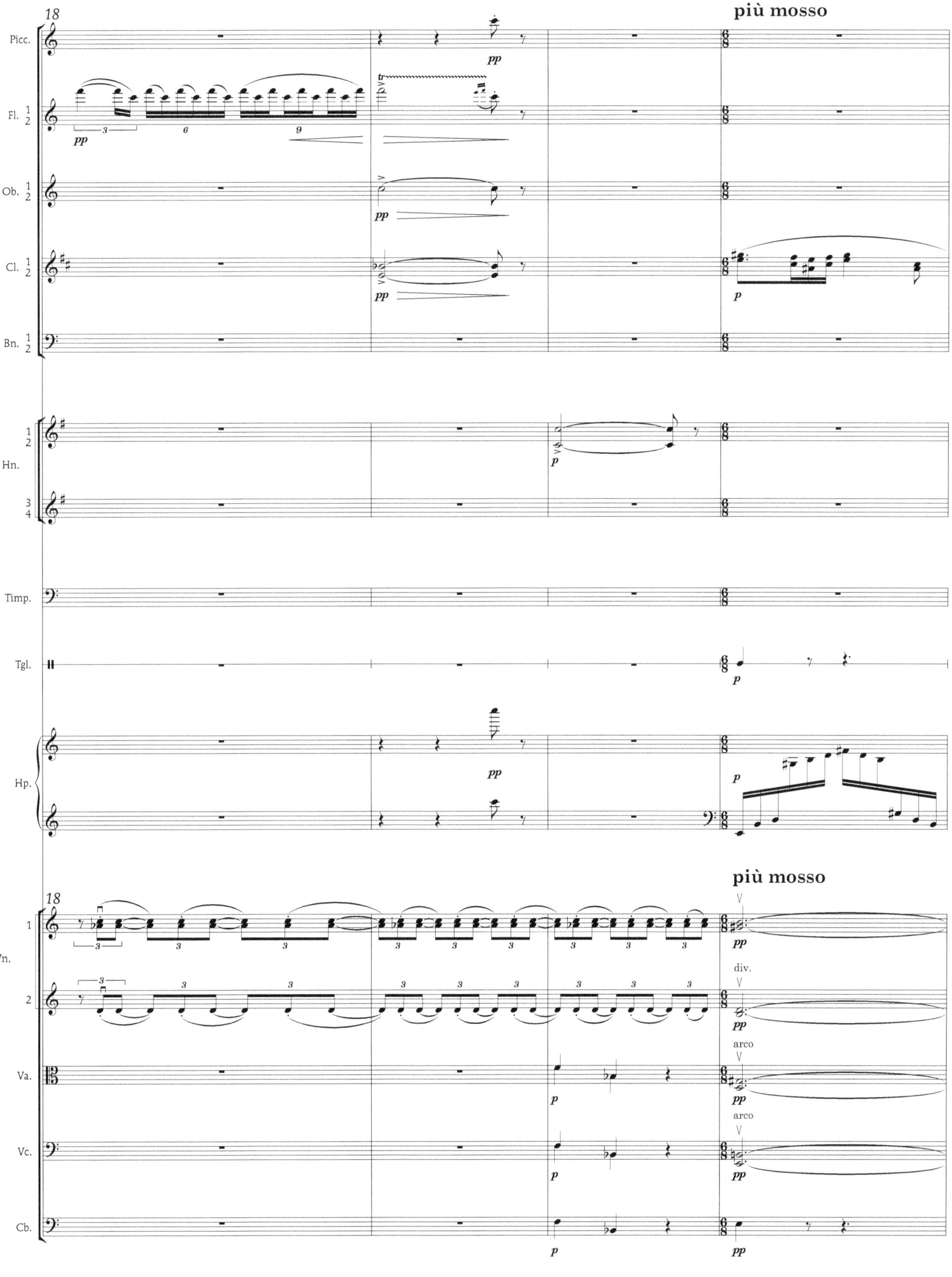
18
più mosso
Picc.
Fl. 1 2
Ob. 1 2
Cl. 1 2
Bn. 1 2
Hn. 1 2
3 4
Timp.
Tgl.
Hp.
18
più mosso
Vn. 1
2
div.
arco
Va.
arco
Vc.
Cb.

22
Picc.
Fl. 1 2
Ob. 1 2
Cl. 1 2
Bn. 1 2
Hn. 1 2 3 4
Timp.
Tgl.
Hp.
Vn. 1 2
Va.
Vc.
Cb.
p
pp
ppp

27
Picc.
Fl. 1 2
cresc. molto
ff
Ob. 1 2
pp cresc. molto
ff
Cl. 1 2
pp cresc. molto
ff
Bn. 1 2
ff
Hn. 1 2
pp cresc. molto
ff
3 4
pp cresc. molto
ff
Timp.
Tgl.
ff
Hp.
cresc. molto
ff
27
Vn. 1
unis.
cresc. molto
ff
2
unis.
cresc. molto
ff
Va.
cresc. molto
ff
cresc. molto
ff
Vc.
cresc. molto
ff
cresc. molto
ff
Cb.
arco
cresc. molto
ff

30
poco rit.
Tempo I
Picc.
Fl. 1 2
Ob. 1 2
Cl. 1 2
Bn. 1 2
Hn. 1 2
Hn. 3 4
Timp.
Tgl.
Hp.
Vn. 1
Vn. 2
Va.
Vc.
Cb.
dim. molto
p
pp
fp
1.

35
Picc.
Fl. 1 2
Ob. 1 2
Cl. 1 2
Bn. 1 2
Hn. 1 2
a2
p
3 4
p
Timp.
Tgl.
Hp.
35
Vn. 1
p
2
p
unis.
Va.
p
unis.
Vc.
p
Cb.

48

42219

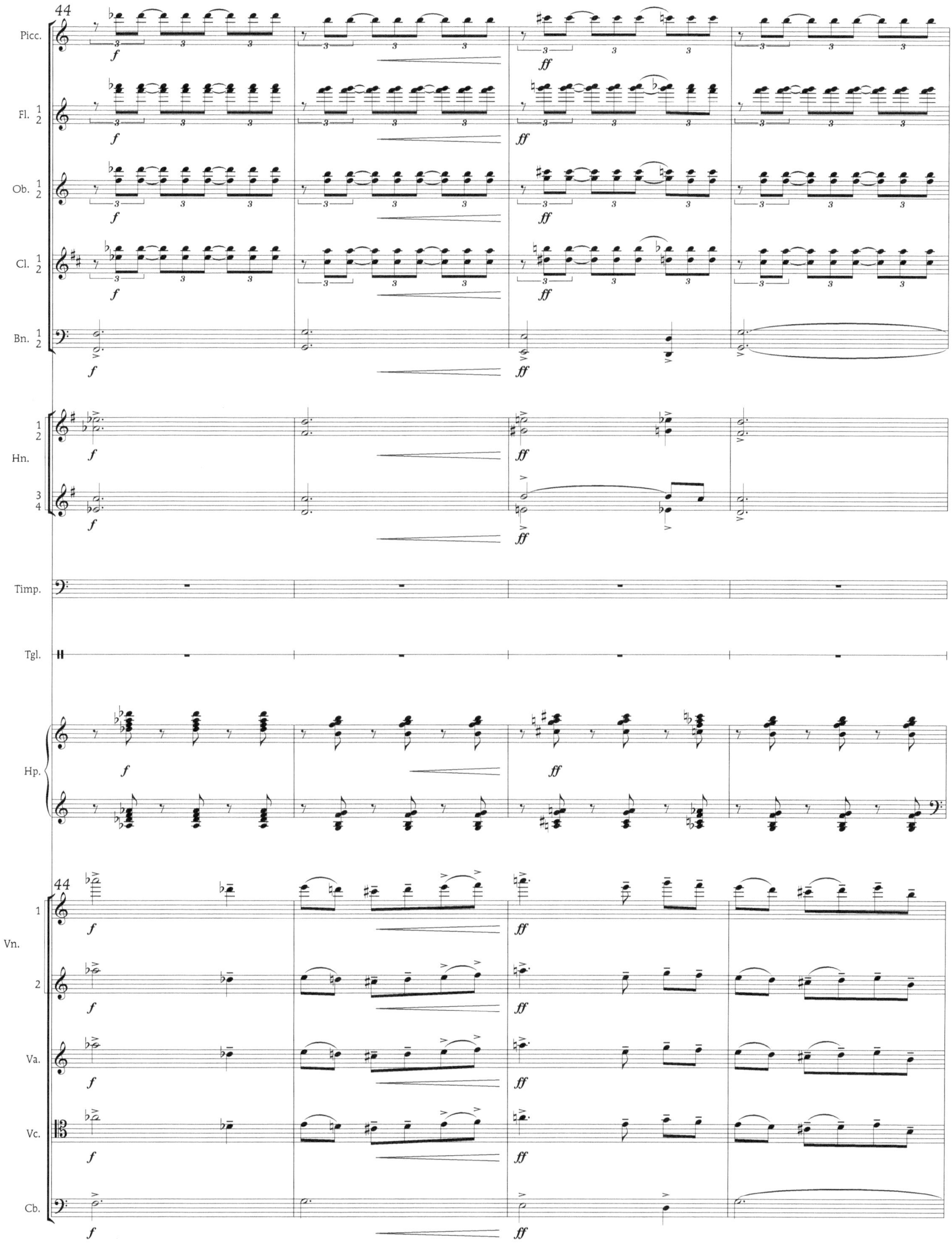
44
Picc.
Fl. 1 2
Ob. 1 2
Cl. 1 2
Bn. 1 2
Hn. 1 2
3 4
Timp.
Tgl.
Hp.
44
Vn. 1
2
Va.
Vc.
Cb.

48
rit.
Picc.
Fl. 1 2
Ob. 1 2
Cl. 1 2
Bn. 1 2
Hn. 1 2 3 4
Timp.
Tgl.
Hp.
Vn. 1 2
Va.
Vc.
Cb.
dim.
p dim.
p
più pp
pp

54
55 Tempo I
Picc.
Fl. 1 2
Ob. 1 2
Cl. 1 2
Bn. 1 2
Hn. 1 2 3 4
Timp.
Tgl.
Hp.
p
mf
54
55 Tempo I
Solo Vn.
Vn. 1 2
Va.
Vc.
Cb.
con sord.
div.
più p
pp
tr

59
Adagio
Picc.
Fl. 1 2
Ob. 1 2
Cl. 1 2
Bn. 1 2
a2
Hn. 1 2 3 4
Timp.
Tgl.
Hp.
molto dim.
Solo Vn.
Vn. 1 2
unis.
Va.
div.
Vc.
Cb.
molto dim.
pp morendo

5.Troldtog
(March of the Dwarfs)

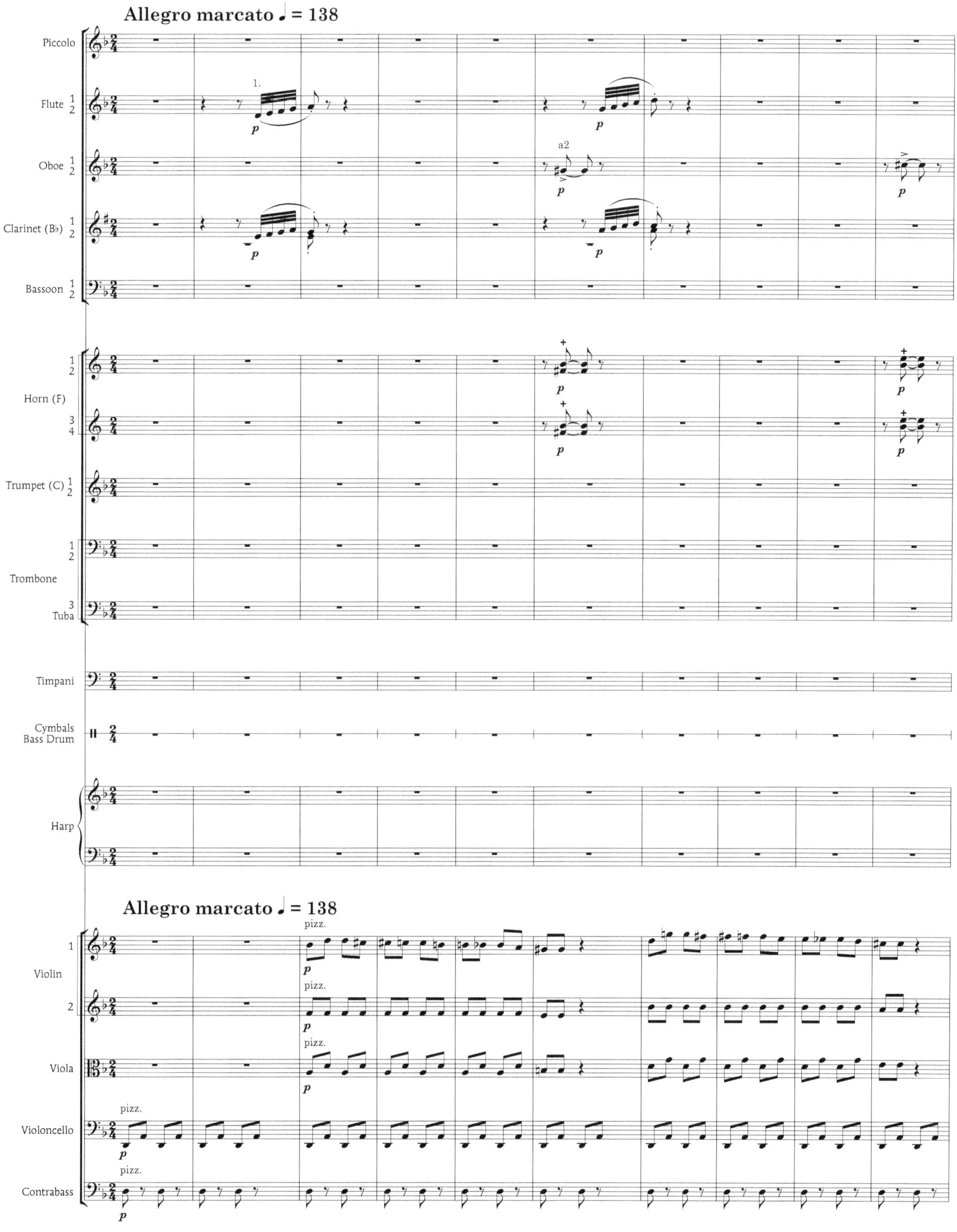

54

42219

19
22
Picc.
Fl. 1 2
Ob. 1 2
Cl. 1 2
p
cresc. molto poco a poco
Bn. 1 2
p
cresc. molto poco a poco
Hn. 1 2
cresc. molto poco a poco
3 4
cresc. molto poco a poco
Tpt. 1 2
Trb. 1 2
3 Tuba
Timp.
Cymb. B. D.
Hp.
19
22
Vn. 1
cresc. molto poco a poco
2
cresc. molto poco a poco
Va.
cresc. molto poco a poco
Vc.
cresc. molto poco a poco
Cb.
cresc. molto poco a poco

56

42219

38
Picc.
Fl. 1 2
a2
Ob. 1 2
a2
Cl. 1 2
Bn. 1 2
Hn. 1 2
Hn. 3 4
Tpt. 1 2
f
Trb. 1 2
3 Tuba
Timp.
Cymb. B. D.
Hp.
38
Vn. 1
Vn. 2
Va.
unis.
Vc.
Cb.

58

42219

51
Picc.
Fl. 1 2
p
dim.
Ob. 1 2
p
1.
Cl. 1 2
Bn. 1 2
pp
Hn. 1 2
3 4
Tpt. 1 2
Trb. 1 2
3 Tuba
Timp.
Cymb. B. D.
Hp.
unis.
Vn. 1
2
Va.
Vc.
Cb.

59
Picc.
Fl. 1 2
1.
pp
Ob. 1 2
Cl. 1 2
1.
pp
pp
ppp
Bn. 1 2
1.
pp
pp
ppp
Hn. 1 2
pp
Hn. 3 4
Tpt. 1 2
Trb. 1 2
Trb. 3 Tuba
Timp.
Cymb. B. D.
Hp.
59
Vn. 1
Vn. 2
(pizz.)
pp
Va.
dim.
pp
Vc.
dim.
div.
pp
Cb.
dim.
pp

poco più lento ♩ = 142

89 Tempo I
82
Picc.
Fl. 1 2
1.
p
3
Ob. 1 2
Cl. 1 2
cresc.
f
Bn. 1 2
Hn. 1 2 3 4
Tpt. 1 2
Trb. 1 2 3
Tuba
Timp.
Cymb. B. D.
Hp.
6
Vn. 1 2
Va.
Vc.
Cb.
unis.
pizz.

93
99 poco più lento
Picc.
Fl. 1 2
Ob. 1 2
Cl. 1 2
Bn. 1 2
Hn. 1 2 3 4
Tpt. 1 2
Trb. 1 2 3
Tuba
Timp.
Cymb. B. D.
Hp.
Vn. 1 2
Va.
Vc.
Cb.
arco
pizz.
1.
p
pp

101
Picc.
Fl. 1 2
Ob. 1 2
1.
p
f
Cl. 1 2
Bn. 1 2
p
Hn. 1 2 3 4
Tpt. 1 2
Trb. 1 2 3
Tuba
Timp.
Cymb. B. D.
Hp.
101
Vn. 1 2
Va.
Vc.
Cb.
arco
p
arco
p
arco
p
arco
p

115 Tempo I
114
Picc.
Fl. 1 2
Ob. 1 2
Cl. 1 2
Bn. 1 2
Hn. 1 2
Hn. 3 4
Tpt. 1 2
Trb. 1 2
Trb. 3
Tuba
Timp.
Cymb.
B. D.
Hp.
115 Tempo I
114
Vn. 1
Vn. 2
Va.
Vc.
Cb.
pizz.
p
pp
1.
2.

121
126 Allegro marcato ♩ = 138
Picc.
Fl. 1 2
1.
p
Ob. 1 2
Cl. 1 2
p
Bn. 1 2
Hn. 1 2
Hn. 3 4
Tpt. 1 2
Trb. 1 2
Trb. 3
Tuba
Timp.
Cymb.
B. D.
Hp.
126 Allegro marcato ♩ = 138
121
Vn. 1
Vn. 2
Va.
Vc.
Cb.
fz
p
(pizz.)

131
Picc.
Fl. 1 2
Ob. 1 2
a2
Cl. 1 2
Bn. 1 2
Hn. 1 2 3 4
Tpt. 1 2
Trb. 1 2 3
Tuba
Timp.
Cymb.
B. D.
Hp.
131
Vn. 1 2
Va.
Vc.
Cb.

139
Picc.
Fl. 1 2
a2
Ob. 1 2
Cl. 1 2
a2
p
Bn. 1 2
Hn. 1 2
p
3 4
p
Tpt. 1 2
Trb. 1 2
3
Tuba
Timp.
Cymb.
B. D.
Hp.
139
Vn. 1
2
Va.
Vc.
Cb.
p

146
147
Picc.
Fl. 1 2
Ob. 1 2
Cl. 1 2
p
cresc. molto poco a poco
Bn. 1 2
p
cresc. molto poco a poco
Hn. 1 2 3 4
cresc. molto poco a poco
cresc. molto poco a poco
Tpt. 1 2
Trb. 1 2 3
Tuba
Timp.
Cymb. B. D.
Hp.
146
147
Vn. 1 2
cresc. molto poco a poco
cresc. molto poco a poco
Va.
cresc. molto poco a poco
Vc.
cresc. molto poco a poco
Cb.
cresc. molto poco a poco

157
155
Picc.
Fl. 1 2
Ob. 1 2
a2
Cl. 1 2
Bn. 1 2
Hn. 1 2
Hn. 3 4
(con sord.)
Tpt. 1 2
Trb. 1 2
Trb. 3 Tuba
Timp.
Cymb. B. D.
Hp.
157
155
arco
arco div.
div.
Vn. 1
Vn. 2
Va.
Vc.
Cb.

162
Picc.
Fl. 1 2
a2
Ob. 1 2
a2
Cl. 1 2
Bn. 1 2
Hn. 1 2
Hn. 3 4
Tpt. 1 2
Trb. 1 2
Trb. 3 Tuba
Timp.
Cymb. B. D.
Hp.
162
Vn. 1
Vn. 2
Va.
unis.
Vc.
Cb.

168
Picc.
Fl. 1 2
a2
1.
p
Ob. 1 2
a2
Cl. 1 2
a2
1.
p
Bn. 1 2
p
Hn. 1 2
Hn. 3 4
Tpt. 1 2
f
f
Trb. 1 2
Trb. 3 Tuba
Timp.
Cymb. B. D.
Hp.
168
Vn. 1
pizz.
p
pizz.
p
Vn. 2
Vn.
pizz.
p
Va.
pizz.
p
Vc.
pizz.
p
Cb.
pizz.
p

174
Picc.
Fl. 1 2
Ob. 1 2
p
Cl. 1 2
Bn. 1 2
pp
Hn. 1 2
3 4
Tpt. 1 2
Trb. 1 2
3 Tuba
Timp.
Cymb. B. D.
Hp.
174 unis.
Vn. 1
2
Va.
Vc.
Cb.

184
180
Picc.
Fl. 1 2
1.
dim.
pp
Ob. 1 2
1.
p
Cl. 1 2
1.
pp
Bn. 1 2
1.
pp
Hn. 1 2
p
pp
3 4
Tpt. 1 2
Trb. 1 2
3 Tuba
Timp.
Cymb. B. D.
Hp.
184
180
Vn. 1
2
Va.
dim.
Vc.
dim.
Cb.
dim.

189
Picc.
Fl. 1 2
Ob. 1 2
Cl. 1 2
Bn. 1 2
Hn. 1 2 3 4
Tpt. 1 2
Trb. 1 2 3
Tuba
Timp.
Cymb. B. D.
Hp.
1.
p
pp
ppp
ff
senza sord.
189
Vn. 1 2
Va.
Vc.
Cb.
(pizz.)
arco
div.
unis.

www.ingramcontent.com/pod-product-compliance
Lightning Source LLC
LaVergne TN
LVHW081321060426
835509LV00015B/1618